States

ALASKA

by Jason Kirchner

CAPSTONE PRESS
a capstone imprint

Next Page Books are published by Capstone Press,
1710 Roe Crest Drive, North Mankato, Minnesota 56003
www.mycapstone.com

Library of Congress Cataloging-in-Publication Data
Cataloging-in-publication information is on file with the Library of
Congress.
ISBN 978-1-5157-0387-7 (library binding)
ISBN 978-1-5157-0448-5 (paperback)
ISBN 978-1-5157-0500-0 (ebook PDF)

Editorial Credits
Jaclyn Jaycox, editor; Juliette Peters, designer; Morgan Walters,
media researcher; Laura Manthe, production specialist

Photo Credits
Alamy: North Wind Picture Archives, 25; Alaska State Library: bottom
18; Capstone Press: Angi Gahler, map 4,7; CriaImages.com: Jay
Robert Nash Collection, bottom left 21; Getty Images: Consolidated
News Pictures, middle 19; Library of Congress: Winter and Pond,
26; Newscom: Design Pics/Jeff Schultz/Jeff Schultz, top 19, DIANA
HAECKER/REUTERS, 29; North Wind Picture Archives: bottom 19;
One Mile Up, Inc: (seal, flag) 22-23; Shutterstock: Africa Studio, top
right 21, akphotoc, 15, Ami Parikh, bottom left 8, B Calkins, 5, Brian
Lasenby, background 9, Catmando, top left 21, Dec Hogan, bottom
right 20, Everett Historical, 12, 27, fon thachakul, Cover, Gail Johnson,
6, 7, gillmar, middle right 21, jdwfoto, middle 18, Jody Ann, bottom
right 21, Joseph Sohm, 13, Lee Prince, 16, M. Cornelius, 14, top left
20, NancyS, 10, optimarc, top 24, Pi-Lens, 11, Ruth Peterkin, 17, s_
bukley, top 18, Steve Bower, middle left 21, thomas eder, top right 20,
tonympix, top right 9, V. Belov, bottom left 20, Vicki L. Miller, bottom
right 8, Zoeytoja, bottom 24; Wikimedia: U.S. Fish and Wildlife Service,
28

All design elements by Shutterstock

Printed and bound in China.
0316/CA21600187
012016   009436F16

TABLE OF CONTENTS

LOCATION...4

GEOGRAPHY 6

WEATHER..8

LANDMARKS..9

HISTORY AND GOVERNMENT.............12

INDUSTRY 14

POPULATION...16

FAMOUS PEOPLE..................................18

STATE SYMBOLS...................................20

FAST FACTS..22

ALASKA TIMELINE 25

Glossary. 30

Read More. 31

Internet Sites 31

Critical Thinking Using the Common Core 32

Index 32

Want to take your research further? Ask your librarian if your school subscribes to PebbleGo Next. If so, when you see this helpful symbol 🖰 throughout the book, log onto www.pebblegonext.com for bonus downloads and information.

LOCATION

Alaska is the largest state in the country. It is not joined to the rest of the United States. Canada runs along Alaska's eastern border and part of its southern border. Water surrounds Alaska on all other sides. To the north is the Arctic Ocean. To the south is the Pacific Ocean. The Bering Sea lies to the west. The narrow Bering Strait separates Alaska and Russia.

Alaska has two long "tails." On the southwest are the Alaska Peninsula, which juts into the Pacific Ocean, and the Aleutian Islands. On the southeast is Alaska's panhandle. Juneau, the state capital, is the major city there. To the south are the Kenai Peninsula and Kodiak Island. Anchorage is Alaska's biggest city. Alaska's next largest cities are Fairbanks and Juneau.

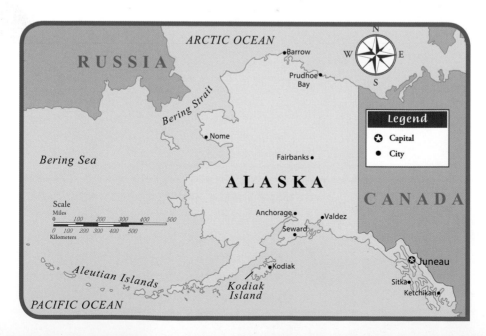

PebbleGo Next Bonus! To print and label your own map, go to www.pebblegonext.com and search keywords:

AK MAP

Juneau is Alaska's largest city by land area, but only third largest by popoulation.

GEOGRAPHY

Alaska can be divided into five land regions. These areas are the Panhandle, the Southcentral, the Alaska Peninsula, the Interior, and the Arctic. The Panhandle is a narrow strip of land between British Columbia, Canada, and the Gulf of Alaska. Mountains and forests cover the Panhandle. It includes islands, inlets, and peninsulas. The Southcentral includes Denali, which is the highest point in North America. The south peak of Denali rises 20,320 feet (6,194 meters) above sea level. The Alaska Peninsula has mountains and volcanoes. Several small mountain ranges spread across the Interior. The Arctic includes flat, mostly treeless plains called tundra.

PebbleGo Next Bonus!
To watch a video about
Wrangell-St. Elias
National State Park,
search keywords:

AK VIDEO

The Columbia Glacier on the south coast of Alaska is one of the fastest moving glaciers in the world.

Denali is located in the Denali National Park and Preserve.

WEATHER

Alaska receives all kinds of weather. The Interior gets warm summers and cold winters. The Arctic is cold and dry. The average January temperature in Alaska is 5 degrees Fahrenheit (minus 15 degrees Celsius). The average July temperature is 55°F (13°C).

Average High and Low Temperatures (Anchorage, AK)

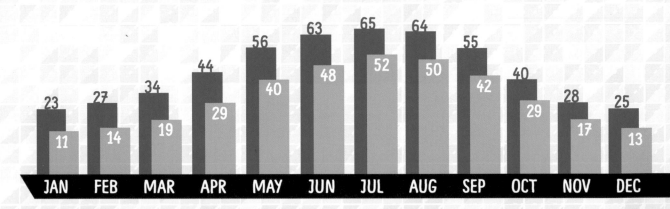

	JAN	FEB	MAR	APR	MAY	JUN	JUL	AUG	SEP	OCT	NOV	DEC
High	23	27	34	44	56	63	65	64	55	40	28	25
Low	11	14	19	29	40	48	52	50	42	29	17	13

LANDMARKS

Ketchikan

Ketchikan in southern Alaska has the largest collection of totem poles in the world. Many totem poles show traditional American Indian spirit figures, such as eagles or bears.

Denali National Park and Preserve

Visitors to the Denali National Park and Preserve in South Central Alaska can view Denali, the highest point in North America. They can see grizzly bears, caribou, Dall sheep, foxes, and moose. Glaciers can be viewed among Alaska's rugged wilderness.

Yukon River

The Yukon River is Alaska's longest river and the third longest river in the United States. It is 1,980 miles (3,187 kilometers) long. This river starts in Canada and flows through Alaska to the Bering Sea.

HISTORY AND GOVERNMENT

When the Alaska Gold Rush started, 100,000 people set out in hopes of striking it rich. But because of the harsh terrain and weather, only about 30,000 actually made it to Alaska.

People have lived in Alaska for thousands of years. The first major groups were Inuit, Aleut, and American Indians. The Inuit lived in the Arctic coastal regions. Aleuts lived on the Aleutian Islands and the Alaska Peninsula. American Indians settled along the southeast coast. Russian explorers were the first Europeans in Alaska. Russia sent explorer Vitus Bering on two voyages in 1728 and 1741. He landed on Kayak Island and claimed the land for Russia. In 1867 the United States bought Alaska. Gold was discovered in Alaska in 1880. In 1912 Alaska became a U.S. territory. Alaska became the 49th state in 1959.

Alaska's government has three branches. The governor leads the executive branch, which carries out laws. The legislature makes laws. It consists of the 20-member Senate and the 40-member House of Representatives. Judges and their courts make up the judicial branch. They uphold the laws.

Alaska's state capitol building is located in Juneau.

INDUSTRY

Alaska's most reliable source of income comes from fishing. Alaska leads the country in fish production.

Crops account for about 60 percent of Alaska's agricultural income. Livestock and poultry products provide the rest.

Crude oil is Alaska's main mining product. Alaska provides almost 25 percent of the oil produced in the United States. Workers in Alaska also pump gas and mine coal, gold, lead, and silver.

Alaska's many service industries, such as health services, schools, and tourism, add to the state's economy. Alaska's many national parks are a popular tourist attraction.

A fishing boat turns into the bay in Dutch Harbor.

Manufacturing is also important to Alaska's economy. Food processing is Alaska's top manufacturing activity. Oil refineries process oil into gasoline. Factories in Alaska also manufacture wood products, such as lumber and paper products.

The Trans-Alaska Pipeline System is one of the largest in the world.

POPULATION

Alaska is the largest state, but it is one of the least populated. Fewer than 800,000 people live in Alaska. Most Alaskans live in cities located along Alaska's coasts or in river valleys. Alaska has several ethnic groups. Roughly two-thirds of Alaskans are white. The next largest group is American Indians and Alaskan Natives. More than 100,000 Alaskans have one of these backgrounds. Alaska has small Asian, Hispanic, and African-American populations.

Population by Ethnicity

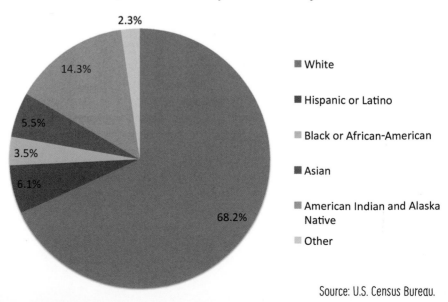

- 2.3%
- 14.3%
- 5.5%
- 3.5%
- 6.1%
- 68.2%

- White
- Hispanic or Latino
- Black or African-American
- Asian
- American Indian and Alaska Native
- Other

Source: U.S. Census Bureau.

The small town of Skagway receives more than 800,000 visitors from cruise ships during the summer months.

FAMOUS PEOPLE

Jewel (1974–) is a singer and actress. Her song "You Were Meant for Me" was a hit in 1996. Her album *Pieces of You* won several Grammy nominations in 1997. In 2013 Jewel released a Christmas album titled *Let It Snow: A Holiday Collection*. Jewel's last name is Kilcher. She grew up in Homer.

Sarah Palin (1964–) became the youngest and first female governor of Alaska in 2006. She was the Republican Party nominee for vice president in the 2008 presidential election. She was born in Idaho and grew up in Wasilla.

Elizabeth Peratrovich (1911–1958) was a Tlingit Indian woman who fought for Natives' rights. Through her efforts, Alaska passed its first antidiscrimination law in 1945.

Joe Redington Sr. (1917–1999) is called the Father of the Iditarod. In 1973 he organized the first Iditarod sled-dog race from Anchorage to Nome. He arrived in Alaska in 1948.

Walter Joseph Hickel (1919–2010) was born in Kansas and moved to Alaska in 1940. He fought for Alaskan statehood and served as governor of Alaska (1966–1969 and 1990–1993).

Joseph Juneau (circa 1826–1900) discovered gold near present-day Juneau in 1880. This led to Alaska's gold rush.

STATE SYMBOLS

Tree

Sitka spruce

Flower

forget-me-not

Bird

willow ptarmigan

Fish

king salmon

PebbleGo Next Bonus! To make a dessert with berries you can find in the wild in Alaska, search keywords: **AK RECIPE**

bowhead whale

Mineral

gold

Animal

moose

Sport

dog mushing

Fossil

woolly mammoth

Insect

four-spot skimmer dragonfly

FAST FACTS

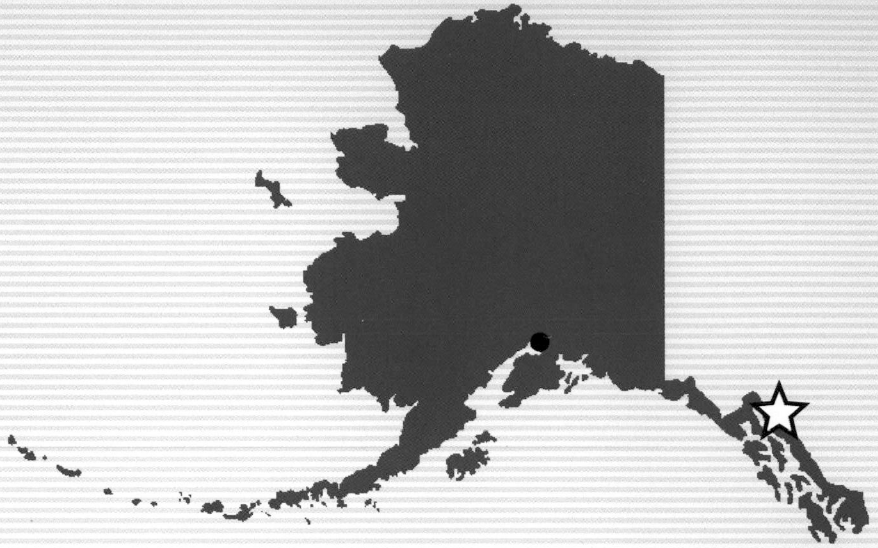

STATEHOOD
1959

CAPITAL ☆
Juneau

LARGEST CITY •
Anchorage

SIZE
570,641 square miles (1,477,953 square kilometers) land area
(2010 U.S. Census Bureau)

POPULATION
735,132 (2013 U.S. Census estimate)

STATE NICKNAME
The Last Frontier

STATE MOTTO
"North to the Future"

STATE SEAL

Alaska's state seal shows a landscape. A smelter symbolizes the importance of mining to Alaska. A train stands for Alaska's railroads. Ships show the importance of sea transportation. Trees symbolize Alaska's forests. A farmer stands for Alaska's agriculture. The fish and the seal on the state seal's outer edge show the importance of fishing and wildlife to Alaska's economy.

**PebbleGo Next Bonus!
To print and color
your own flag, search
keywords:
AK FLAG**

STATE FLAG

Alaska's state flag has eight gold stars on a field of blue. Seven of the stars are in the shape of the Big Dipper. It's one of the constellations in the night sky. It stands for Alaska's strength. The eighth star is the North Star. It stands for Alaska's future and the state's position as the northernmost state.

MINING PRODUCTS

petroleum, zinc, natural gas, gold, lead, silver

MANUFACTURED GOODS

petroleum and coal products, food products, nonmetallic mineral products, fabricated metal products, transportation equipment, computer and electronic products, printing materials

FARM PRODUCTS

milk, eggs, poultry, beef, hay, potatoes, vegetables, barley, decorative plants

PebbleGo Next Bonus!
To print a copy of the state song, search keywords:
AK SONG

ALASKA TIMELINE

1620 The Pilgrims establish a colony in the New World in present-day Massachusetts.

1741 Explorer Vitus Bering sails to Alaska, claiming it for Russia.

1783 The American colonies win independence from Great Britain in the Revolutionary War (1775–1783).

1784 Russians establish the first white settlement in Alaska on Kodiak Island.

1861–1865 The Union and the Confederacy fight the Civil War.

1867 The United States buys Alaska from Russia.

1853 The U.S. Congress creates Washington Territory.

1880 Miners Joseph Juneau and Richard Harris discover gold near present-day Juneau in southeastern Alaska. Alaska's gold rush begins.

1899   Gold is discovered in Nome in western Alaska.

1912   Alaska becomes a U.S. territory.

1939–1945   World War II is fought; the United States enters the war in 1941.

1942   During World War II Japan attacks the Aleutian Islands in western Alaska.

1959 Alaska becomes the 49th state on January 3.

1968 North America's largest known oil field is found in Prudhoe Bay in northern Alaska.

1971 The Alaska Native Claims Settlement Act returns land to Alaska's native people. The act gives $962 million and 44 million acres (18 million hectares) of land to native Alaskans.

1973 The first Iditarod sled-dog race is held. The race starts in Anchorage and ends in Nome. It covers more than 1,000 miles (1,600 km).

1977 The Trans-Alaska Pipeline opens. The pipeline transports oil 800 miles (1,287 km) from Prudhoe Bay in northern Alaska to Valdez in southern Alaska.

1989

The *Exxon Valdez* tanker hits a reef, spilling millions of gallons of oil into Prince William Sound, which is part of the Gulf of Alaska. It is one of the biggest oil spills in U.S. history.

2001

The Special Olympics World Winter Games are held in Anchorage. The event attracts more than 10,000 people.

2006

Sarah Palin takes office as Alaska's first female governor.

2014

Dallas Seavey wins the Iditarod Trail Sled Dog Race across Alaska in record time. In 2012 25-year-old Seavey became the youngest musher to ever win the Iditarod.

2015

President Obama renames Mt. McKinley to Denali.

Glossary

agriculture *(AG-ruh-kul-chur)*—the science of growing crops

economy *(i-KAH-nuh-mee)*—the ways in which a country handles its money and resources

executive *(ig-ZE-kyuh-tiv)*—the branch of government that makes sure laws are followed

industry *(IN-duh-stree)*—a business which produces a product or provides a service

inlet *(IN-let)*—a narrow bay of water that juts inland

legislature *(LEJ-iss-lay-chur)*—a group of elected officials who have the power to make or change laws for a country or state

peak *(PEEK)*—a pointed top

peninsula *(puh-NIN-suh-luh)*—a piece of land with water on three sides

poultry *(POHL-tree)*—farm birds raised for their eggs and meat; chickens, turkeys

region *(REE-juhn)*—a large area

rugged *(RUHG-id)*—rough and uneven, or having a jagged outline

smelt *(SMELT)*—to melt ore so that metal can be removed from the rock

voyage *(VOI-ij)*—a long journey

Read More

Bjorklund, Ruth. *Alaska*. It's My State! New York: Cavendish Square Publishing, 2016.

Felix, Rebecca. *What's Great About Alaska?* Our Great States. Minneapolis, Minn.: Lerner Publications, 2016.

Ganeri, Anita. *United States of America: A Benjamin Blog and His Inquisitive Dog Guide*. Country Guides. Chicago: Heinemann Raintree, 2015.

Internet Sites

FactHound offers a safe, fun way to find Internet sites related to this book. All of the sites on FactHound have been researched by our staff.

Here's all you do:

Visit www.facthound.com

Type in this code: 9871515703877

 Check out projects, games and lots more at
www.capstonekids.com

Critical Thinking Using the Common Core

1. Alaska is not joined to the rest of the United States. How might its location affect how people travel there? (Integration of Knowledge and Ideas)

2. Fishing is Alaska's most reliable source of income. What other industries are important to Alaska's economy? (Key Ideas and Details)

3. Alaska is one of the least populated states. Why do you think so few people live in Alaska? (Integration of Knowledge and Ideas)

Index

Alaska Peninsula, 4, 6, 12

Aleutian Islands, 4, 12, 27

Arctic, 6, 8, 12

capital, 4, 22

Denali, 6, 10, 29

economy, 14–15, 23

ethnicities, 16

famous people, 18–19

farming, 14, 24

gold rush, 19, 26

government, 13, 18, 29

Gulf of Alaska, 6, 29

history, 12, 25–29

Interior, 6, 8

Kodiak Island, 4, 25

landmarks, 9–11

   Denali National Park and

     Preserve, 10

   Ketchikan, 9

Yukon River, 11

manufacturing, 15, 24

Panhandle, 4, 6

population, 16

size, 4, 22

Southcentral, 6

state symbols, 20–21, 23

weather, 8